DATE DUE

Demco, Inc. 38-293

Clem Maverick

CLEM MAVERICK

The LIFE *and* DEATH *of a*
Country Music Singer

BY R. G. Vliet, *1929-*

WOODCUTS BY
Barbara Whitehead

Shearer Publishing   Bryan, Texas

Shearer Publishing
3208 Turtle Grove
Bryan, TX 77801

The author is grateful to the following for their previous association with this work: *The Texas Quarterly*, the Viking Press, Earplay, The Corporation for Public Broadcasting and National Public Radio.

The lines on pages 36 and 37 from "I've Got a Hole in My Pocket" by Felice & Boudleaux Bryant are © 1958 by Acuff-Rose Publications, Inc., and reprinted by permission of the publisher. The quotations on the frontispiece and on page 36 from "It's Better to Have Loved a Little" by Hank Thompson are © 1952 by Brazos Valley Music, Inc., and used wtih the permission of the author and the publisher.

ISBN 0-940672-13-8

First Edition

Printed in the United States of America

Thamus, are you there? When you reach Palodes,
take care to proclaim that the great god Pan
is dead.

It's great to be king in glory
Even tho you have to fall
HANK THOMPSON, *singing*

He shouldn't of never
of died. Never.

Clem Maverick

Today in the capital it's Clem Maverick Day.
High-stepping, white-crotched majorettes gambol.
Corps of twirlers prance away,
tails snapping in the sun like shrimp for gumbo,

boots cut tall and skirts cut short.
The entire legislature's adjourned for the day
to watch the apple-kneed twirlers sport
as twenty-seven hand-picked schoolbands play

Dixie and Aggieland and Semper Fidelis.
Today in the capital it's Clem Maverick Day,
the governor a-saddle, the queen in her trellis,
the thousand-gallon stetsons of paper maché,

the rose-wove floats of Texas-size guitars,
the cowgirl duchesses in bannered cars.
The whole damn crowd just stomps and roars,
and tonight there'll be a host of recording stars.

These hand-dyed fancybelts cowboy-tooled,
these beltbuckles pounded, turquoised and diamonded,
these sand-bellied roll-brimmed 7X beavers
with leather hatbands,
this ruby-horned saddle to ride his finger,
this silver fiddle for his lapel, these leather
ties, silk ties, Windsors, gamblers, hand-painted
sequined four-in-hands,

these rainbow britches, these spangled blouses
with the pearl snaps, these tall-up and silver-toed,
hand-carved and fancy-foxed veal and sharkskin
cowboy boots,
these dove-gray, canary-yellow, rhinestoned and satin-
    lined,
ranch-cut in Hollywood, cockleburr
and Texas rose, doeskin gabardine
hillbilly suits,

this flat-top guitar that stopped many a beer bottle
in honky tonks, and when he'd gone high class
this big blonde nickel-plated eight-stringed
electric—*everything here but his great
blue yodel.*

Please do not lean on the glass.

 III

At thirteen
stuck his flattop in a towsack
and turnt pro.
Set up this threepiece combo
with me and Leon to back
on banjo
and bullfiddle and we was mean,
man, mean—
ah ha San Antone you oughta seen
us go.

I sung
backseat and Clem would yodel
up a storm.
I tell you it got warm
when we pulled out the throttle.
Clem
Maverick and His Cowboy Kings.
Wingdings,
hoedowns, county fairs, auctionings,
barn

4

dances, rodeos,
medicine shows and forks in the road.
Clem couldn't
of told you a music note
from a cowtrack, but he was good.
Folks wrote
in letters. We was on the radio
at Del Rio.
That night Clem yodeled from his toes
up. Had to tote

him from the mike.
Then come the honkytonk years.
That's a place
to dance some and mainly to raise
a row. Try to hear your ears
in that ratrace.
The crowd so all-fired thick
a puredee stick
couldn't stir it. And then to pick
a bass

5

fiddle
in all that beer and ruckus?
But one high
old Saturday night we done "I
Got the Word," Clem's first famous
song. *Whoo-ee*,
they went hogwild in the middle—
Clem busted a window
going, but lit singing and a little
sky high.

6

 IV

I rid on down to Kern's
with the devil in my head
I said I'd have my darlin
or leave her old folks dead
Lordy that sun. But now werent
that a turrible thang to do? In that song
I mean.
      Mmmm-mmmm Mmmm-mmmm
      and off her hand took five gold rings
      bowee down dee
      Come tonight there'll be a breeze
on the Plateau. It always does. I use
to could lay on my pillow of a night and pick
song ballets out of it, it goes so sweet
and mournful.
      Mmmm-mmmm Mmmm-mmmm
        Hand me them other snapbeans.

That's
his daddy you hear out there in the thicket.
I never seen such a big-veined man. Oh,
and when he comes in he talks so loud
from the weather. He's nigh eighty. He caint
barely straighten his fingers from the ax.
But he's always chopped cedar. A man's
got to live, aint he? I mean live.
Sometimes them cedar needles puts such
a sweetness acrost his neck. And I fix
him beans and red-eyed gravy.

Onct that man
pulled a fiddle like dipping honey from a bee
tree. Now how could a lonesome gal
deny a one like that?
leaf by leaf the roses fall
drop by drop the wells run dry
That's a dwellin
song and ought to be dwelt on the long
notes.

Looky that hawk in his stoop
up yonder. Aint that a wonder?

I suppose
you want to hear about Clem. He give
us this place. Course this country aint worth
a damn exceptin to hold the world
together. And for cuttin cedar posts.
But that cedar lasts. It lasts
like bone.
Hold this basin a minute
I got to shift some.
I had eight
sons and Clem was one. He came way
late. He was so *wrinkled* when he come,
like on the neck of a sheared goat.
I never did know what to make
of him. Him and Cade. They was a pair.
And Buckle got tall enough to climb
on a horse. But no taller. There was Lee
and little Rudy. How the sun used to turn
in that boy's tow hair. And Ransom
and Johnny.
All gone but them last
two now.
So many chicks about
my skirts! So many chicks.

9

                              And I had one
daughter onct. Name of Augusta.
I aint never lost her face. I tell you
it'll take the steers of Hell to drag her
from my breath. Her dear small breath
I kissed it. She was perfect of light
and gentleness. It was a Wednesday she
took sick. She turnt such shining
eyes and fever cheeks. She burnt
along her hair. Days and days. She fair
went like kindlin. Then got so strange
and peaceable, like settlin of ashes and past
her hurt. Wanted up from bed. She said,
Mama it's so *light*. Her pore daddy
helt her thin as sticks in his arms
and she said, Put on my bonnet. I put
the little fresh muslin bonnet
on her head. She werent but five. I said,
Gussie do you want to see God? Yes
Mama. Do you want to see Rudy? Yes . . .
Mama.
              O Jesus got up. Got up
from the grave. Pulled off them grave
clothes. Shaken off the girdles, taken
the napkins from his chin and laid
them in the grave.
      in that shining land above

10

But it's Clem
you're intristed in. Onetime down the Nueces
we was after pecans. Clem climbed black branches
to give the tree a shake, but it come
a rotten branch. Clem's arm never
did set right. It's how come
he helt his guitar so peculiar.
          and now my song is over
          I will sing to you no more

V

His face was dark as Mexico
and gun-blue was his hair
and he has cleared two acres of thorns
and one of prickly pear,
one of prickly pear.

The wife she stood by the kitchen shade
the rancher he stood at the door
"I've no use for you to finish my lots
and you owe me for beans and more,
you owe me for beans and more."

"Don't go today my husband dear
for to burn your pile of thorns
I dreamt I heard the cruelest song
from the dark side of the moon,
the dark side of the moon."

She had not sat from the locking of her doors
to combing back her yellow hair
when who should she see at her own window
watching her across his guitar,
watching her across his guitar?

She had not gone quite from the room
not quiteways down the stairs
when who should she see at the bottom of the steps
with catclaw and cedar in his hair,
catclaw and cedar in his hair?

"What o what do you want with me?
What do you follow me for?"
and she mounted brisk and she took three coins
and she flung them to the floor,
she flung them to the floor.

Then he took out his long penknife
he was fairly up the stairs
and he knifed her until her own heart's blood
ran down her milk white knees,
ran down her milk white knees.

He has made across the yard
and across one stony acre
where greenly grows the live oak tree
and sweetly sings the mocker,
sweetly sings the mocker.

14

He leaned his back against the oak
he moaned above his guitar
it was the highest hour of day
but the brush smoke it climbed higher,
the brush smoke it climbed higher.

He sung *mejicano* until he heard at his back
the husband and five tall neighbors
and he rested there and he waited there
and sweetly sung the mocker,
greenly grew the live oak tree
and sweetly sung the mocker.

 VI

Sure I knowed Clem Maverick.
We growed up together. Come acrost
his first guitar hangin in a live oak.
Him and me that night was hot
after ringtails. Thought we'd treed
a ringtail sure. What we treed
was a old flattop guitar. But that's
a long story. Nothin a stranger'd
be intristed in.
                    Learnt his chords
off a old nigger sheepshearer name
of Freejo. Blackest nigger
I ever did see. That nigger
had lightnin under this thumbnail. Fair
lit up a guitar. "Git away
fum me, boy. Git away fum me
wid dat ol wetback guitar." Clem
dogged his tracks. I'd a-been scairt
my ownself.

Freejo hadn't
but three lefthand fingers. Ever
notice how Clem helt his guitar
so queer? Well his three-fingered
chordin was a sight queerer.
                                                 Hell,
in them days all Clem and me
ever give a good goddamn for
was huntin and to pick a sweet guitar.

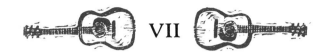 VII

Blue who ooo what'll I do
money's all gone what'm I comin to
and call me lonesome your wranglin heart
blues baby blues since we been apart

ah odle lay-hée   dee-o-dle lay-hée
dee o-dle lee-dle lo-dle lay-hée heee hee
dee-odle lay-hée-hee   lay hée-hee
dee-odle lay-hée-hee   dee-lay héee

my head tall up my heart low down
sunalong baby gonna leave this town
catch me a catcherful of mockerbird song
baby maybe you got me all wrong

cause a Saturday Sunday ever night
gotta be where the lights are bright
sunalong lord I'm on my way
catchin the midnight turnin day

ah odle lay-hée   dee-o-dle lay-hée
dee o-dle lee-dle lo-dle lay-hée heee hee
dee-odle lay-hée-hee   lay hée-hee
dee-odle lay-hée-hee   dee-lay héee

 VIII

Pan piping his oattunes. "Sunalong,"
"Sugarbabe," "Five Miles from Dallas,"
"When the Great Day Breaks." Clem
was real country. Picked his guitar
with a cactus sticker. Likely had ringtails
grinning in his hair. *I caint*
read a note except in my heart.
But he could sew a song together
with a red hot needle and a burning
thread. His headpiece was crammed with suchlike
ditties. Used to fetch them to me
scribbled on tobacco-wrappers and envelopes.
And sing? Could sing skywide, noodle
a note, drag a moansome vowel
hitch it in mid-note and crack
it across his tonsils—*I wu-under.*
Pan. O Pan. He'd ramble
up into a yodel all high yonder
like a scissortail swung on a wind
off cedar, suck that word love
off the roof of his mouth, his guitar just
a-blinking. He really meant it. It was
the wild and the lonesome and the hurt. Some
angel must of pinched his hillbilly nose

19

to make him sing so pure mournful.
Here was a real troubadour. I inked
him a pact with TopNotch Music.
I lined him out on the rustic circuit.
It was what he wanted. But o
you Goatboy, horns hung
in the branches.

O you jukebox warbler.

 IX

Once he came to the Palace.
I saved out of my lunch money
for it. And first LulaBelle
came on and she was funny

and the Westerly Trio but we
wanted Clem Maverick.
When we heard his guitar
it got quiet quick.

His guitar played so sad
prettier than on the radio
and he begun to sing
baby-o baby-o baby-o

and walked into the light.
I shivered in my knees.
It made you want to squeal
and kick your feet and squeeze

him like a little boy
he was so lonesome cute.
I got all his records.
I got a whole suit

of drawers full. Without
"Sugarbabe" and "Blue No More"
I couldn't stand to work
all day in this dimestore.

X

When does hillbilly
                    get to be Country
Music, honey?
                    When you can wear
a mink like this.
                    I know it's June.
They're nice to drape
                    across a chair.
I got lots more
                    right upstairs.
Like I say
          Clem was always
sweet to me.
                    All his lovesongs
was writ to me.
                    We knowed
true love.
          Maybe in a minute
we could go up
                    and looky them others.
My mink I mean
                    and maybe show
you all my purty
                    cowgirl dresses
I got up there?

                        You probably heard
I aimed to be
                a singer once.
I went to see
                Big D Stompede
and maybe audition
                        and Clem seen me.
He weren't but eighteen
                        myself just a mite
touch older.
                We was hitched
next night.
                That fixed me
as competition.
                He wrapped my voice
in a dirty apron
                and made damn sure
it stayed in the house.
                        Not really.
I'm only kidding.
                Honey if we
was to go upstairs
                we might could see
some of Clem's things.
                        I keep 'em locked
up sacred.

Or maybe you'd like
to come set here.
                    You want to know
how-all Clem wrote.
                    He'd listen a minute
and then start picking.
                    He use to say
if he couldn't get it writ
                    in half an hour
he'd toss it away.
                    Sweetie this talking
curdles my throat.
                    Pretty please
just a dribble.
                    Not too much.
Clem weren't all
                    so great as they say.
If TopNotch Music
                    hadn't juiced 'em up
they wouldn't of been
                    a single hit.
Me and Misery
                    Me and Misery
that's how it went
                    the whole damn day.

And amiddle the night
                    to get stab awoke
by a morbid song
                    name of "Blackjack"—
mostly about
                    burning arms
and eyesocket smoke?
                    I bet you never
heard *that* on wax.
                    It came from there:
that cedar-panel room.
                    He'd set in there
starknaked on the floor
                    but for a pair
of cowboy boots
                    and all that hair
ever light
          switched on bright
head throwed back
                    eyes scrunched tight
slamming a beatup
                    Meskin guitar
and singing "Blackjack."
                    "Leave me be.
Leave me be.

They's a scab on the sun.
I got black crickets
                        chawin my back."
This was a dude
                        with dark in his fingers
from the word Go.
                        I think his body
was turning to stone.
                        He'd take off
on the Hamburger Tour—
                        Dallas Fairgrounds
San Francisco Cow Palace
                        Seattle, Toronto
those thimble-breasted bitches
                        climbing all over him
the whole damn way.
                        But all Clem's lovesongs
was writ to me.
            All Clem's lovesongs
was writ to me!
                        O
get the hell
            get the hell
GET THE HELL
            OUT OF HERE!

28

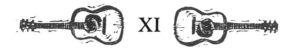 XI

I recollect about twict a year
or so he use to haul into town
wearin one of them there silk
tablecloths on his neck. Drove
two creamcolored convertibles equipped
with I don't know what-all: sunshades
unbornt calf, white leather
upholstery. Like he'd just hove
smack through some herd of milk
cows or other. He kept
a Spanish mansion off the square.
White. I reckon you found it
easy enough. The kings of Egypt!
You'd a-thought he wore a crown
sure. Lordy, the kings of Egypt!
But we was talkin about the weather.
I tell you, if I ever see a blade
of grass again, I'll walk around it.

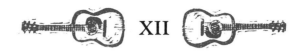 **XII**

Met him in Salina, Kansas.
"Come on down to the coast with me.
I got a boat in Port Aransas.
I got *two* boats in Port Aransas."
I was packed in nothing flat,
ditched my classes at the University,
headed for Texas just like that

in his air-conditioned car. Outside
Ardmore, Oklahoma, once, we stopped
to watch some leggy colts alongside
the road. They leaned to their mothers' sides
and ran through the short, windy grass.
It was the only time we stopped
other than for drinks and gas.

Below Waco we outdrove a twister
and a Texas Ranger, Clem singing. He
said I had yellow hair like his sister.
I don't think he even had a sister.
Also we never got to the coast.
Ended up in a State Fish Hatchery
smack against a cypress and almost

out there swimming with the fish.
As it was we were up to our gills in liquor.
We counted the moons with beards of Spanish
moss snagged and tugging in the cypress
branches. The hood was littered with moonchunks.
About that time the plot got thicker.
Clem was chasing me around tree trunks.

One place I pressed to a tree tight.
I might have been cedar except I was giggling
and except a mockingbird was scattering its bright
different-colored music right
above—lark, catbird and phoebe.
Then I was scared as anything,
and Clem caught me under the tree.

It was some hairy wrestling. Without
his stetson he was almost bald. He had
a dimple like a scar next his mouth. I caught
a taste of it. It turned out
all he wanted was me to ride
on his back. Can you imagine? I fed
the bastard some grass and got astride

him and whipped him with a grassstem
through the night air. We didn't get far.
He fell asleep. The bronco Clem
at Churchill Downs. I left him
and Man o' War in the vodka pastures
and followed my clothes back to the car
to pick the damn moss and cedar

sticks from my hair. I don't know
what kind of footprints we left behind.
I waited until it began to grow
light and watched the scissortails plow
their breasts into the watertop
and flutter up new from the pond.
Clem Maverick was still asleep

naked in the wet grass, his
wiry body-hair strung with dew.
I got my things and caught a bus
home. There. That's all there is.
It's enough. You see why you're
hearing this by phone? And don't try to
contact me. I won't be here.

 XIII

Towards the last
already half off his bronc from whisky
his outfit splotched with sequins and sweat
they'd have him propped in the wings, the fiddler
covering with a fast

fill-in, and ready
him up and hand him out to the stomping
and whistling. He'd stare a minute at the mike
up to his knees in electric cords
and about as steady

as a wet calf
his rhinestones blinking, his guitar swinging
off some gulch, and finally pull back
stifflike and tell them to go to Hell.
They'd just laugh.

And tell them
to go get their money back, he weren't
going to sing. They'd clap. Then the steel
guitar'd whip out like a pistol shot
and snap him

up onto his silver
toes, rope him into a deadpan dance.
He'd jerk inside his gabardine, pop
along his backbone like somebody cracking
dry cockleburrs

give a hitch
a shiver to shake the wind from his feathers
and would he pick! would he yodel!
longgone, buddy, his gullet full of wild
and cedarback scratch

like he'd never been curried
below the knees, his Cowboy Kings
coming in behind him like a Baptist
choir, the electric steel slamming
through the brush, lead

guitar pecking
in amongst the peppercorns, kicking
up a dust, the sweetgums high in the trees
the old bull fiddle down
in the backseat necking.

They wouldn't let him quit.
It crowded your ears to hear them holler.
He'd try to flat out, his Spanish guitar
crying, picking over the ruins
but they wouldn't let him quit.

With the audience on the prod
out front, it got to the point where I
refused to follow Clem on a show.
Don't throw *me* to the wolves, I'd say.
I ain't iron-shod.

35

 XIV

Don't tell me how it was, good buddy.
I played fairy godmama to him.
In my various roles of blowfly and hounddog
and cockleburr (to use his words), I
was always under his skin or on his tail
or in his hair, one. LulaBelle the prize
retriever. My job was to shoo Clem
off the bottle in time for the next show.
He was prone to pack a playful pistol
back of his belt. My job was, when he
was done dusting out his hotel room,
to go in and settle up the costs
and see they didn't sue. I reckon I knew
Clem good as any. He poured ketchup
on ever'thing he et. Yep, and one minute
be bawling like a baby at a purty sunset,
next minute up on his hocks rampaging,
stomping a wad of money into the floor.

Once in Los Angeles when he was blue
and dry and looking to get hisself soaked,
we kept him all afternoon in a car. We done
the sights and took him down Sunset Boulevard.

He tried hard to be cooperative. "Well,
let's sing," he said. We begun "When the Great
Day Breaks," which was his favorite hymn.
Of a sudden Clem let out this animal screech.
He flung his head onto my lap
like some knotted bony old broken fist
and sobbed, "It's done broke.
It's done broke. *And they ain't no light.*"

Lordy, like the saying goes: hillbillies
drive the longest cars and wear
the biggest diamonds and the flashiest clothes
and the raggedest underwear.

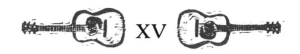 XV

In March that year
when half the Panhandle
was freighting across the sky

the sun a brown
smidgin there and our teeth
gritty and sinuses dripping

with spring in the air
he come sure-enough blue
on a cracked sidewalk in Waco.

In the hospital outside town
he sprung his tubes and siphons
and greened-up and died.

His blood was laced
with Old Crow and Seconal
and mescaline and they put it down

to a heart attack
at age 29. The last word
they think he said was *August*

but let's face it
it don't make sense. The nurses
cleared away the gear

and let him go back
to his brushcountry ranchtown
down on the Plateau where they

raise pricker
bushes and mohair. The local
Chamber of Commerce rigged

him a floral
thigamajig of guitars and memory
pillows in front of the courthouse.

The crowd was thicker
than crickets to the funeral.
The Chuck Wagon Gang

led with a choral
job of "Beyond the Sunset."
It was going on the wind.

Folks cried.
They really cried when Tex Jones
sung "When the Great Day

Breaks." It looked
to be a wet Mardi Gras.
Women fainted. Flashbulbs

lit and died
like Clem hisself. And I got
the word. Now they really

got him booked
up solid. Now they really
got him down on wax.

40

 XVI

For Christ sake should he of been
some thin ditty along
some fencerow? A piece of piping
under mountain laurel? Thistle music
off in the brush or what might
dance on a rock by night if you
could prove it any by this knot of hair
snagged to bobwire? There sure
wouldn't of been no cash in that.

41

XVII

We wore long black
stockings then
                    and here's
me.
        And here's Clem
way in the back
                        row
like he was trying to hide
behind weeds.
                    He looks
sort of rabbit-eyed.
That's just like him.

I remember his carved
                            sloped
desk
        fitted him best
for sleep and how I
didn't like him then.
Until at recess once
some boys with pencils and sticks
were teasing a hummingbird

                              caught
in a web
            beating
                    like a piece
of green
        fire
                like a satiny
daymoth thing. All
green
        and red
                    and yellow
and Clem let it go.

Then it was different.

Clem taught me how
to whistle on a piece
                        of panic
grass
        and I let him
copy out my lessons
and yes onetime at lunch
we split a whole
                    lard

bucket
        full of green
wild
        huisache
                        honey
he'd climbed a bluff for
down the Nueces
                        and were
were
        were
                we sick.
Now he's yonder
                        under
the rock squirrels.

                        Let's go
outside. But look. Even
then
        there was something old
about him.

                        Let's go out.
Supper's cooked. Jim

ought to be up from the pens
directly.
            We could wait
under that big
                live oak
and then all three walk back
to the house.

            Clem never
hurt nobody but himself.

Watch you don't skid
on the acorns
                when we get there.
It's been a high dry year.
Still and all the ground
is drenched with
                acorns.
                        We
might can see
                some late
goldeneyes and maybe see
goldfinches in the brushpiles
                        there.

45

Jim and me
            just bought
this ranch. We hope to do
right well. But for years
nobody's kept the place.
I mean, not to *live*.
Oh
    they'd lease the sections
for browse right enough
but that's all. There was some
trouble
        here
                a long
while
        back. Yes that's
a mocker. He'll do
                it over.
And look
        at those
acorns.
That live oak puredee *thrives*.

 XVIII

Another minute and we're on the wind.
Soon as Ma's Real Old-Fashioned

gets in her licks, then one
more plug for cold Lone

Star. Here we go. This opener
ranchero's what I call a roper

  I hate to see

it throws your heart. Old Clem
warbles it like it was hurting him.

  it end

A TopNotch platter. The other side's
the splinter-kicker. Since Clem died

  so sudden

he's took off from the hillbilly division
gone Top Ten across the nation

47

sprouting on jukeboxes everywhere. Yessirree
if they could peg Clem's dirty laundry

Have a little

at 45 RPM and spin it
man there'd be a fortune in it.

fun

It's like a white-eyed horse turned loose
raring and rampaging and tearing across

tonight

the countryside and folks chunking coins
at it to hear it screech. If anyone

tells you Clem's dead that's a crock.
Take it from this old disk jock.

48

 XIX

goodnight sweet prince

DEAR CLEM,
               we got the word
by phone you've gone away
bound for Home on the Glory Train
to a Brighter Day.

Dallas is pretty far
from Him in His Judgments There.
The Big Boss of the Roundup likely
wanted you near.

Now you're in Hillbilly Heaven.
Oh what a star-studded Land.
You'll write for the greatest singers Clem.
The Angel Band.

49

You'll broadcast from the Holy Station.
You'll purely pick your guitar.
The Heavenly Music will make us look
to the Western Star.

You'll sing again you see.
They'll do you Up Yonder in style.
Still and all we're glad you sung
our way awhile.

Rest in Peace. May
your songs Clem Maverick
make *His* Top Chart.
                    Sincerely,
                            WE
AT TOPNOTCH MUSIC.